HOW TO PAINT OWLS

A Guide to Materials, Tools, and Technique

David Mohrhardt

Stackpole Books

Published by
STACKPOLE BOOKS
Cameron and Kelker Streets
P.O. Box 1831
Harrisburg PA 17105

Printed in the United States of America

10 9 8 7 6 5 4 3 2 1

First Edition

Cover and series design by Tracy Patterson

Library of Congress Cataloging-in-Publication Data

Mohrhardt, David.
    How to paint owls : a guide to materials, tools, and technique /
David Mohrhardt. — 1st ed.
        p.   cm.
    Includes bibliographical references.
    ISBN 0-8117-2243-0 : $24.95
    1. Owls in art. 2. Watercolor painting—Technique. 3. Gouache
painting—Technique. I. Title.
ND2280.M63   1990
751.42'2432—dc20   89-39929
                                                            CIP

To
Foster, Katherine, and Helen,
and in memory of Delmar

Contents

Introduction

 Owls are the most recognizable and popular of all birds. They have been the object of attention for centuries, and their image has been reproduced on everything from coins to Christmas ornaments to bed sheets. All this popularity is despite the fact that owls are reclusive and seldom seen. No one knows precisely why people have this fascination with owls, but it is theorized that their popularity stems from their apparent stoicism and from their humanlike facial appearance, with eyes at the front of the head, "eyebrows," and a bill that corresponds to a nose. Whatever the reason, owls are a definite favorite with the public.

The challenge in painting owls is not just to capture them physically in paint but to portray the essence of an individual owl's expression, whether it is sleepy-eyed, bored, surprised, or whatever. Thus to paint owls properly is no small feat. Their basic coloration is usually muted, and the feather patterns may be intricate and difficult to discern. Their breast feathers have a soft, puffy look that takes time and practice to render properly. And, of course, owls have certain physical characteristics peculiar to them that must be taken into account.

This book will examine each aspect of owls and of painting in detail, then will show you how to combine materials, techniques, anatomy, colors, and attitudes to create an expressive and accurate owl painting.

1
Painting
Mediums

Many mediums may be used in bird painting; however, two in particular—gouache (opaque watercolor, designers colors) and acrylic—are used more frequently and with greater success by most wildlife artists. These two mediums, although dissimilar in some respects, are alike in others. They are both water-soluble, have good covering ability, dry rapidly, and may be used opaquely or transparently.

Oil paints and transparent watercolors are beautiful mediums but do not lend themselves easily to bird painting. Oils require oil solvents as a thinner, are rather thick to work with, and dry quite slowly. They may be used thinly, but this technique requires a great deal of experience. The newer water-based "oil" paints are thinned by water but work in a manner similar to traditional oils. Conversely, transparent watercolors are applied very thinly and dry quickly. Their great disadvantage is their inherent transparency, which means that it is hard to cover one color with another and mistakes are difficult to correct.

A word of caution here: whichever mediums you choose to work in, keep in mind that many of the pigments used are toxic or carcinogenic in one degree or another. This does not mean that under normal conditions painting is hazardous to your health; it merely means that you should use common sense. After painting, wash your hands before eating or smoking, or any time there is excess paint on your hands, because some toxic materials may be absorbed through the skin. And *never* point your brush by putting it in your mouth.

You can purchase a wide variety of premixed colors, but it is wise to get only a few basic ones (red, yellow, blue, green, black, white, raw umber, burnt sienna), work with them, and then buy additional colors as needed. Whether you are a beginner or an expert, painting is easier with a limited palette.

Color mixing in any medium is almost an art in itself. It would be best to familiarize yourself with the basics of colors and color mixing by getting a beginner's book on color theory and then experimenting, blending colors to obtain the best results for you. When you obtain a desired color, either while experimenting or while involved in a painting, make a note of which colors were mixed to obtain that color. Never trust your memory; later you may attempt to duplicate a particular color and be unable to do so. Making color notes is tedious but worthwhile.

Gouache

Gouache is the easiest medium to work with because of its forgiving qualities; its opaqueness allows mistakes and corrections to be made and the paint remains workable even when dry, permitting blending and scrubbing out of colors.

Gouache may be used thinly to give a very transparent color, layers of color may be allowed to build up, or it may be used in a completely opaque manner with darks over lights, or vice versa. Whichever effect you choose, it is accomplished with the addition of water to the concentrated pigment. However, gouache should not be used too thickly or it will crack.

The dry gouache paint has a matte, nonglossy finish and great visual weight. It is available in a wide variety of colors, but, as with most pigments, the degree of *light-fastness* (permanence) can vary widely. Most color charts have a key which indicates the light-fastness of the various colors. The ratings are: (E) Excellent; (V) Very Good; (G) Good; and (F) Fugitive. For art that is to last, it would seem folly to use any colors below the Very Good rating.

Not only does the permanence of color vary, but same-named colors from different manufacturers can have very different color values, especially in the earth tones. The best approach is to familiarize yourself with the color differences between the brands via color charts, which are available free or at a nominal cost from the manufacturers or art-supply stores, then choose the colors and brands you are most comfortable with.

When you look at the color charts you will notice the great variety of shades of the basic colors (reds, yellows, blues, etc.), but don't ignore the blacks, which have color characteristics all their own. *Ivory* (bone) *black* has a brownish tone, *lamp black* a bluish tone, and *mars* (jet) *black* is a deep velvet black. When mixed with other colors or white they give very different results.

Gouache may be purchased in tubes, cakes, or jars, with tube gouache being the most readily available. The paints in tubes and jars remain workable over a long period of time as long as the caps are kept securely in place. The key is to keep air away from the paint, especially in tubes where the paint is more viscous to begin with. After squeezing needed paint from a tube, whether transparent watercolor, oil, acrylic, or gouache, never squeeze the sides of the tube to suck the paint back in—this only allows excess air into the tube and accelerates drying in the tube. With gouache and acrylics it is advisable to put the colors on the palette only as you need them because they will dry out on the palette. The gouache may be worked when dry, but acrylic will dry completely, rendering it useless.

A shortcoming of gouache is that because it remains water-soluble even when dry, it is possible for a color already painted on a picture to bleed through into another color being applied over it if the second color is worked too much with the brush. Even when dry, the surface of gouache will rub off slightly with vigorous movement, so it is advisable to place a small piece of paper under that part of your hand that is touching the art so that traces of color already applied are not picked up and dragged around.

Despite the minor disadvantages of gouache, it is still the most versatile and easiest medium to use in bird painting on flat surfaces and is the first choice of beginners and experts alike.

Gouache Mediums

Gum arabic is the basic binder used in the manufacture of gouache. It is also used, in small quantities, to increase the transparency of gouache and impart a slight gloss to the normally matte finish. It is most commonly available in small jars.

Ox gall is made from the bladders of oxen. This natural wetting agent is the best material to increase the uniform flow of gouache, particularly in washes. Only small amounts are used, and it is available in small jars.

Acrylics

As mentioned previously, gouche and acrylic have much in common: rapid drying time, water solubility, opaque or transparent use. But there the major similarities end. While both are suitable for painting on flat surfaces, acrylics are best for painting birds in the round, whether wood or clay. The basic color selection of acrylic is not as broad as gouache, and is only available in tubes and jars. Again, color charts should be consulted for the variety of colors available. The consistency of the paint in tubes and jars is quite different: the paint in jars is less viscous and easier to thin to a flowing or brushing consistency.

One of the difficulties a beginner encounters is achieving the proper working consistency for acrylics. Whereas gouache cannot be used thickly, acrylic may be used from a transparent wash to a thick impasto; obviously, the working consistencies can vary widely. A rather disconcerting quality of acrylics, especially for beginners, is that even though they may appear to be opaque and dense on the palette they work very thinly on the painting surface and it may take two or three applications of color to achieve a solid color, if indeed that is your intent. There is no formula; only experimentation and experience will teach you the right "feel" for the particular painting being done.

The short drying time of acrylic paints cannot be emphasized too much simply because when acrylics dry, they are *dry*: they become extremely hard and are not water-soluble. This means that wet-in-wet blending between colors must be done while the paints are still workable; however, a blended or shaded effect may be achieved if a graded wash is put on over an already dry color (see Techniques). The hard nonsoluble surface is a distinct advantage when applying glazes (thin washes of other colors) or other solid colors over an already painted surface since the paints will not bleed into one another. The surface of dry acrylics will not rub off, thus your painting hand won't drag colors around.

Acrylics have excellent permanence and may be used on virtually any surface. A ground coat of gesso is necessary on many surfaces, especially canvas, wood, and clay. The colors have great visual weight and look juicier and brighter than gouache; the surface of the dry paint has a slight sheen.

The big precautionary note for acrylics is that, because of their rapid and hard drying qualities, care must be taken to clean brushes and other tools immediately after use because dry acrylic is virtually impossible to remove from many surfaces, including clothing and floors.

Initially acrylics seem difficult to control, but don't be dismayed by first attempts—work with them until you've mastered their use. They are a valuable and versatile medium, whatever the painting surface.

Acrylic Mediums

Acrylic retarder is a gel that retards the drying time of acrylic paint. It is usually available in tubes. Care must be taken to add the proper amount of retardant to the paint; the instructions on the container should be followed.

Acrylic flow release is added to acrylics in small amounts to reduce the surface tension, thus increasing the flowability and permitting more even washes on paper or paperboard.

Acrylic gel medium is a thickening material that not only allows an impasto effect to be achieved, but makes the paint more transparent. It has very limited uses in bird painting.

2
Brushes

Almost any hair, bristle, or fiber may be used in the manufacture of brushes for painting, and all have different characteristics. The brush is the most important tool in bird painting. There is nothing more frustrating or self-defeating than trying to work with a poor brush. Purchase the highest quality brush(es) you can afford. Don't be dismayed at the array of shapes and sizes; only a few good brushes are necessary for successful bird painting.

What determines a good brush is a combination of abilities: to carry an adequate load of paint, to hold a sharp edge in a flat brush, to hold a sharp point in a round brush, and to spring back into shape after use. Emphasis here will be on the materials and shapes used most frequently in bird painting with gouache and acrylic paints.

Types of Hair and Filament

Kolinsky Sable. The finest and most expensive brushes made are from Kolinsky sable, but even these will vary in quality depending on the manufacturer. Kolinskys are typically found in the round shape and usually display all of the desirable qualities of a good brush. Although there are many brands, the two I recommend for availability and consistent quality are the Strathmore series 585 and the Winsor & Newton series 7.

Red Sable. Sable hairs that are of a lesser quality than Kolinsky: usually they are not as springy and in rounds do not point up as well as Kolinskys. In other shapes—flats and filberts—they are fine brushes.

Sableline. A fancy name for dyed ox hair. They do not point up well in the rounds, but they can hold a good load of paint and are fine flat and large wash brushes.

Nylon. Sometimes designated as synthetic sables, nylons have great spring but little ability to point or hold paint. The development of synthetic filaments has not yet achieved the quality found in natural hair brushes.

Blends. The most common blend is nylon-sable, and although a better brush than pure nylon, it is still lacking in paint retention and the ability to hold a fine point.

Shapes of Brushes

Standard Round. Usually just called a "round," this is the most popular and versatile shape, found in a variety of sizes. Though this is called a *standard* round, various characteristics such as hair length may vary between manufacturers. The two most popular brands are Winsor & Newton and Strathmore.

Designer Round. These have a longer, thinner shape than standard rounds and come to a narrow, sharp point that can pull a very fine line. This is a good style but not quite as versatile as the standard round.

Flat. There are two categories to be considered in this style: watercolor and oil flats.

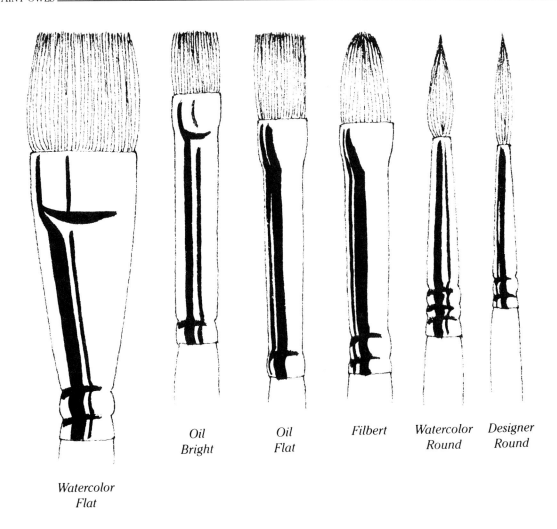

Oil
Bright

Oil
Flat

Filbert

Watercolor
Round

Designer
Round

Watercolor
Flat

Brush Shapes

Watercolor Flats. Initially, this brush category may seem confusing since watercolor flats may also be called *aquarelles*, which are large, thick flats, or one-stroke brushes which usually have slightly longer hairs than normal flats. Regardless, they are all watercolor flats and all are used primarily for washes or filling in large areas. They are generally not found in very small sizes, and the most common sizes are ¼, ⅜, ½, ¾, and 1 inch. Red sable and sableline are the preferred hairs in this shape; lesser-quality brushes in this shape have a ragged edge, don't hold much paint, and have the annoying habit of losing hairs when painting. Another brush to be considered here is a large flat called a *wash brush*, used, as the name implies, for putting washes on large flat surfaces. A good large wash brush is the 1½- or 2-inch Oxhair by Strathmore.

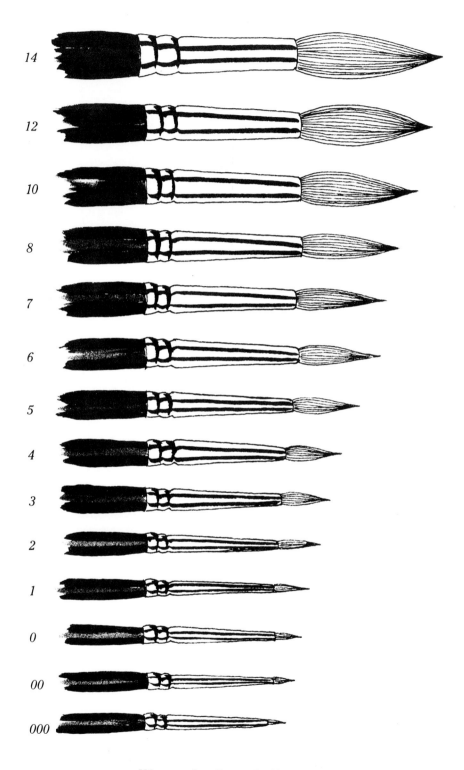

14

12

10

8

7

6

5

4

3

2

1

0

00

000

Watercolor Rounds (Actual Size)

Oil Flats. These come in a much greater variety of sizes, have shorter hairs, and are more stout than watercolor flats. Oil flats are used for oils and acrylics on canvas or wood. The *bright* is another flat but with slightly shorter hairs than the oil flat.

Filbert. This is a flat but with a rounded rather than a square tip. Traditionally regarded as an oil-painting brush, it is now an important shape for painting birds in gouache and acrylic as well. Used in an unconventional manner it produces unique featherlike marks (see Techniques). The various sizes of this brush make different sizes of feather marks, so which size you will need will be determined by the size of the bird being painted. The different types of hair in this style make different types of marks. Red sable would be the best hair choice to start with, but be sure to experiment with other types of hair and bristle.

Care of Brushes

Several brushes may represent a considerable investment and it is wise to care for this investment with the small amount of time it takes to keep brushes in good condition. Cleaning water-based paints from brushes only requires rinsing them thoroughly in body-temperature water, then gently scrubbing them with a pure soap such as Ivory bar soap. After rinsing all the soap out, reshape the tip of the brush and hang it hair- or bristle-down to dry. When you are using several brushes it is difficult to stop painting and clean them. In cases like this, there is a piece of equipment called a brush washer or brush holder. It is merely a container of water with a coiled-spring metal holder mounted above the water level. When the brush handle is put in the coil, the hairs may be suspended in the water, keeping the paint in the brush moist until it can be washed out thoroughly.

If you have extra brushes or some that are used infrequently, store them in a closed—but not airtight—container along with some moth crystals (moth larvae love to munch on hairs and bristles). With proper care some brushes may last a lifetime, but even if the ends wear off they are still useful (see Techniques).

Buying Brushes

The ideal way to buy a brush is to go to an art-supply store where you can test the brush before buying; it is especially wise to test sable rounds of any quality. Testing merely involves wetting the brush in water to remove the manufacturer's starch (used to protect the brushes), then, when it is thoroughly wet, flick the brush quickly to see if it points well. After that, press the damp hairs sideways on a hard surface and release them to see if the brush snaps back into shape. If the brush behaves well, buy it; if not, repeat the performance with another brush. Oftentimes it is necessary to order brushes from a mail-order company. Just stick with reliable brands and you will usually be pleased. If not, most firms have a complete return policy.

The recommendations here are to be used only as a guide. All artists have individual preferences and the best way to satisfy your artistic needs is to experiment until you find which brushes are best for you.

3
Painting
Surfaces

Although many surfaces may be painted on, only those widely used with gouache and acrylic will be discussed here. **Watercolor Papers** are available in a wide variety of weights, finishes and shades of white and gray. The following is an overview of the terms used to describe watercolor paper and its characteristics.

Watercolor paper is commonly available in three finishes, or surface textures, although the degrees of texture on same-named finishes differ widely from one manufacturer to another. These papers are available in rolls, pads, and individual sheets. Although watercolor paper is intended for use with transparent watercolors, gouache may be used on it with great success; however, it is not recommended for the inexperienced acrylic painter.

Hot Press is the smoothest surface and will take very fine line detail and is used mainly for hard-edged paintings. The surface has very little "tooth" (roughness to the fiber) to hold paint, which has a tendency to lift off the paper at inopportune times.

Cold Press is the intermediate finish between hot press and rough. With a moderate surface and tooth, it is the finish of choice for the beginning artist.

Rough is, as the name implies, a very rough finish, and because of this is a very difficult surface to work on. It is an attractive surface but does not lend itself well to detailed paintings.

Watercolor paper is listed by weight as well as finish, and if the paper dimensions are the same, the higher weight will be thicker paper. Size is

Watercolor paper surfaces. From the left: *Rough, Cold Press, Hot Press*

important because the standard is based on how much a ream (500 sheets) weighs, no matter what the size. Thus a larger sheet of the same thickness will be listed at a greater weight.

Most lighter-weight watercolor papers must be stretched prior to use to avoid buckling. This is a simple process. Soak the paper in a pan or tub of water, remove the paper when thoroughly wet, and drain off excess surface water. Then place the wet paper on a flat surface, such as a drawing board, and tape the edges all around using a gummed paper tape. Tack the corners through the tape and let dry. The paper will dry very tight and may be used taped to the board or cut free. Stretching is not necessary with heavy-weight watercolor papers.

Illustration and Watercolor Boards are stiff boards with either illustration paper or watercolor paper adhered to one side. Because of the stiffness, these boards can stand rougher treatment than papers and do not require any prepainting preparation.

Illustration board is lighter in weight than watercolor board and has a slight tendency to warp when large areas are painted. To remedy this problem, merely brush a thin coat of gesso or paint on the reverse side to equalize the pull of the paint, thus flattening the board. Illustration boards are available in two surfaces, *hot press* and *cold press*; the hot press is the smoother and less desirable of the two. Cold press provides good surface for both gouache and acrylic.

The difference in thickness between Illustration Board (left) *and Watercolor Board* (right).

Watercolor boards are made with a heavier backing than is illustration board and thus are more resistant to warping. Since the surface is watercolor paper, it responds well to paint. The three surface finishes are the same as those already described for watercolor paper. The preferred watercolor board is Crescent #114 cold press, a very heavy board with Strathmore watercolor paper adhered to it. Gouache and acrylics may be used with great success on this fine board.

Matboards are constructed of tinted paper adhered to stiff backing. There is a temptation to use this board for painting, and it can be done; just be aware that the tinted paper fades to a great degree.

Hardboard, commonly known under the trade name Masonite, is made of compressed wood fibers and is found in tempered and untempered forms. Only the untempered board should be used for painting because the tempered board is impregnated with oil. Prior to painting, the board must be coated with acrylic gesso to provide a suitable ground (surface) for the paint. Preparation with gesso requires rolling or brushing a base coat of thinned gesso, then sanding with a fine sandpaper and dusting and applying more gesso, repeating the process till at least three coats of gesso are on the surface. The reverse side of the board must also be coated but need not be sanded. This offsets the board's tendency to bow by creating surface tension on the reverse side. Gouache may be used on hardboard panels but only with limited success. Acrylics work well on hardboard but it does take some patience, because initially paints go on the slick gesso surface rather irregularly. However, after additional applications of color the painting goes smoothly. A finished acrylic painting on hardboard is very crisp and bright.

Primed linen canvas

Canvas. Both linen and cotton are referred to as canvas and both are available in different grades and weaves, the tighter weaves being the more expensive. Gouache may be used on canvas, but acrylics have much greater success. Because of the inherent texture of the fabric, canvas does not lend itself easily to fine-line paintings—except for the portrait linen canvases.

Cotton canvas is available in several forms: rolls, panels, pads, and pre-strehced; the form most suitable for painting with acrylics is the prestretched, acrylic-primed canvas. Found in a wide assortment of sizes, these canvases are ready to use and easy to store. The surface of cotton canvas can be rather coarse, with irregularities in the weave.

Linen canvas is more tightly woven, stronger, smoother, and more expensive than cotton canvas, and is available only in rolls or prestretched and primed. The latter is preferred for our purposes. Because of the weave and stability, linen canvas is the preferred choice of most artists because its fine surface permits detailed paintings.

Wood panels historically have been used for painting surfaces; however, the concern here is not for wood panels but for carved wood used by modern bird carvers. Finished carvings must be primed to accept the paint and to provide a white ground that enables colors to be crisp and clear. Wood must first be sealed with clear lacquer or sanding sealer, then one or two coats of acrylic gesso, thinned to the point where it will not fill in carved detail, is brushed onto the surface. When dry, this provides an excellent ground for acrylics. Gouache is not suitable for carvings because of its soft surface.

Primed cotton canvas

Additional Mediums, Tools and Accessories

Just a peek inside an art-supply store or catalog is enough to bewilder any artist. Besides the array of brushes, paints, and paper, there are myriad accessories and gadgets, some useful—some not. Listed here are only those additional art items which are necessary for successful bird painting.

Liquid Masking Fluid (Liquid Frisket) is a thin rubber-cement-like fluid that is painted over an area to be left white after painting washes or specific areas. Use a worn-out or inexpensive brush to apply the frisket because it dries and balls up in the brush quickly. Immediately after use, wash the brush in water. When the background color is completely dry, the frisket is removed by gently rubbing off with the finger(s) or with the help of a rubber cement pickup. Liquid frisket is used extensively in bird painting (see Techniques). I recommend Winsor & Newton tinted liquid masking.

Palettes may be made of metal, plastic, paper, china, wood, or glass. Some have wells to hold the color, and some have lids to keep the paint moist. Despite the variety available, the best palette is usually the simplest, and anything that will hold paint may be used. Most acrylic painters prefer something that is peelable or disposable like an old plate, pizza pan, or hardboard scrap, and a pan with a shallow lip or enameled tray is ideal for gouache.

Transfer Paper is a thin paper coated on one side with graphite; it is used to transfer a drawing to another surface. It is available commercially or may be easily made by first rubbing a thin coat of graphite from a soft pencil or graphite stick on one side of a piece of tracing paper or on the reverse side of a drawing, then smearing the graphite around with a tissue to get a more even coating. To transfer a finished drawing to the painting surface: prepare the back of the drawing as described or place a piece of transfer paper between the drawing and surface, trace over the lines of the drawing, remove the drawing, and the traced lines are transferred to the painting surface. This acts in the same way as carbon paper does, which, incidentally, should not be used for drawing transfers because carbon paper smears badly and is difficult to erase. If the transfer is to be made onto a dark surface that will not show graphite, smear the back of the drawing with silver- or white-colored pencil instead, and white lines will be transferred.

Brush Washers or *Holders*, as mentioned previously, are handy and inexpensive pieces of equipment.

Water Jars hold the water used for diluting paints and washing brushes while painting. From hand-thrown pots to canning jars, anything that will hold water will do.

Spray Bottles are used for the even prewetting of surfaces. Trigger types are superior to pump types; they may be purchased empty at hardware stores and beauty shops.

Sponges, both natural and artificial, have a variety of surface textures and are used for special effects as well as for controlling water and washes.

Hobby Knives (X-acto types) are used in painting for scratching white lines on painted surfaces and for carefully removing unwanted hairs, paint flakes, or whatever may suddenly appear on a painting.

Tissues, Paper Towels and *Rags* are always handy for removing excess paint or water and for blotting paint from brushes.

Q-Tips provide a ready-made instrument for blotting small areas of paint, as in lifting off (see Techniques).

4
Techniques

All the basic techniques shown here apply to gouache; however, not all apply to acrylics, because when dry, they cannot be reworked. Though every effort is made to indicate how the techniques are executed, it is difficult, it not impossible, to describe the precise consistency of a paint, wetness of a wash, or amount of pressure on a brush. These are variables that can only be learned through experience. Even veteran artists keep a scrap of board handy while painting to continually check for consistency, color, load of paint in the brush, or to practice line shapes. Don't be discouraged—these techniques are easy to master through practice. It is important, once you have mastered the techniques, not to overuse them. Learn when to stop.

Flat Opaque Colors—Dilute the paint to a creamy consistency and, using the appropriate-size brush for the area being filled, use broad strokes to fill in with opaque color. Acrylics may require two coats to cover completely.

Wet-in-Wet Wash—This technique is used for backgrounds or on the bird painting itself, wherever a continuous, even, transparent color is desired. For a large background wash have a puddle of thinned paint ready to go, then place the board on a slight angle so the water and then the paint will flow slowly and evenly down the board. Wet the board surface thoroughly so that it shines, then, starting at the top of the board and working downward, brush on the thinned paint from side to side, adding paint and brushing until an even wash is obtained. If the first wash is too thin, wait until it is completely dry and then repeat the process. When working a small area on a bird, wet only the area to be colored and brush carefully. The paint will brush evenly into the premoistened area, giving a beautiful, thin, even coat.

Graded Wet Wash—The preparation is the same as for a wet-in-wet wash; the difference is that the brush is charged with paint only once, and as

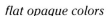

flat opaque colors

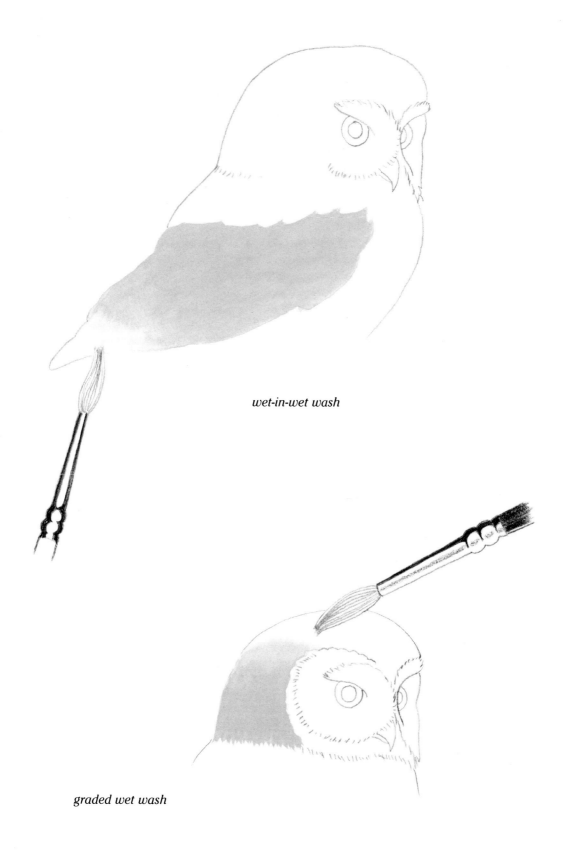

wet-in-wet wash

graded wet wash

the brush works down the board there is less and less pigment, thus the effect is a graded tone. Often after the initial color to be graded is applied, it is washed down the surface with a clean damp brush. This is a very useful technique in bird painting, especially for achieving a shaded effect in acrylics by grading a wash over a base color (glazing).

Wet Blending—Paint two areas of color close to each other on a damp surface and work the edges of each color into the other while still wet until a blended effect is achieved. This technique may be used with acrylics but you must plan ahead and work quickly, while the paint is still wet.

Dry Blending—Easily done with gouache but not possible with acrylics, this is, quite simply, blending two adjacent dry colors with a clean, damp brush. Use a light touch on the brush and move it back and forth across the edges of the colors until they are coarsely blended, then brush along the edge to achieve a smooth blend. This is very handy for softening the edges of thin lines as on wing edges.

Glazing—This is an application of a thin wash of color over an already dry one, allowing the colors to mix visually. A graded wash painted over a base color is an example of glazing. Acrylics lend themselves beautifully to this technique but care must be taken with gouache not to overwork the second color on the surface or the colors will bleed together.

Drybrush—Though this technique is rarely used on the bird image itself, it is frequently employed on the supports (twigs, logs, and so on). The

wet blending

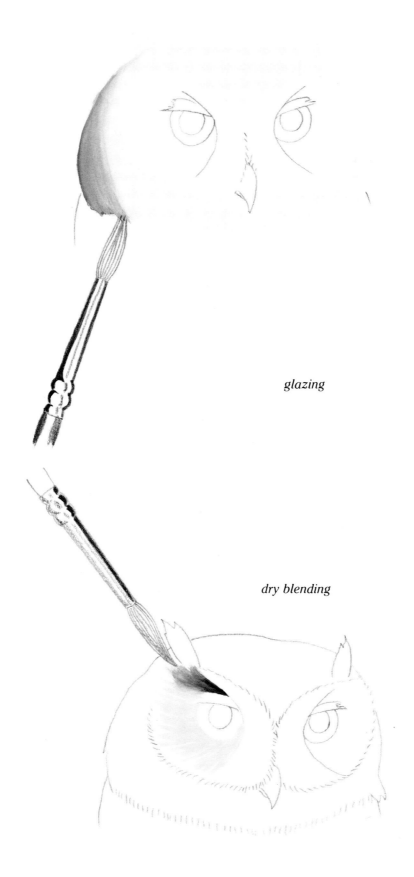

glazing

dry blending

brush is charged with color, blotted until almost dry, then dragged across the surface, creating an unpredictable broken, shaded effect. The tip or side of the brush may be used.

Splitbrush—Also known as *heeling* or *feathering*, this is a versatile and fun technique, and one that invites overuse. A round brush is charged with paint and severely pinched or pressed down at the heel (where the hairs and ferrule meet) until the hairs spread apart. Then the tips of the spread hairs are brushed lightly across the surface, making a series of tiny lines. The brush may be blotted to produce drybrush broken lines. A graded or blended effect may be achieved by using a series of light short strokes on the edge of a color. Short light splitbrush strokes are a very effective way to soften the edge of wet acrylic paint, producing a blended effect. Be warned that this is very hard on brushes; old, worn brushes are recommended.

Tipping—The filbert-shaped brush is most effective for tipping, and care should be taken not to overuse this technique. The brush is not held in the conventional manner, like a pencil, but rather, is held almost parallel to the surface, but at a slight angle. The brush is charged with paint and the tip is lightly pressed to and then lifted from the surface. Varying amounts of paint, degree of pressure, or a pressing-then-pulling motion, all produce a wide variety of featherlike marks.

Lifting Off—Rather than adding color to the surface, this is a subtractive technique for removing color (it cannot be done with dry acrylics). A brush filled with clean water is lightly scrubbed over a selected area of dry paint. While the area is still wet, a Q-tip or clean, dry brush is used to lift the loosened pigment from the scrubbed area. This leaves a subtle highlighted area, the shape and size of which is determined by the motion of the wetted brush.

drybrush

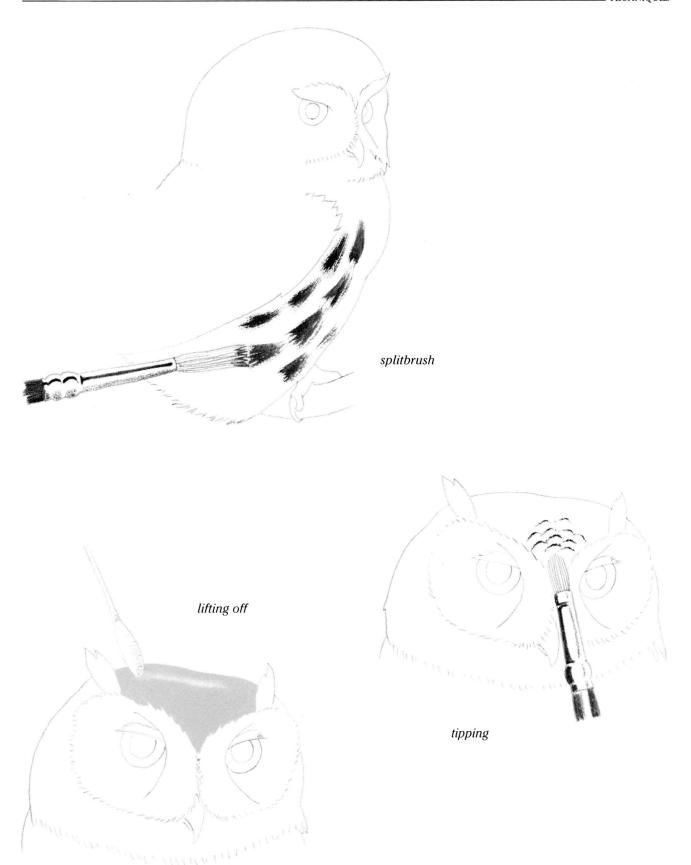

splitbrush

lifting off

tipping

Detailing—Usually the last technique used on a painting, this is the addition of finishing detail, usually employing a small fine-point round brush. In bird painting, the wing edges, highlights, and other finishing touches are described as detailing.

Spatter—This technique is not used on the bird but rather on the background to suggest an irregular sandlike surface. It is accomplished by dipping an old toothbrush in very thin color, then lightly rubbing the bristles of the toothbrush with a stick or finger. As the bristles snap back and forth, random-sized dots of color appear on the painting. Both light and dark colors may be spattered. To control the area being spattered, frame it with a piece of torn paper; this will give a varied, more interesting edge to the spattered area.

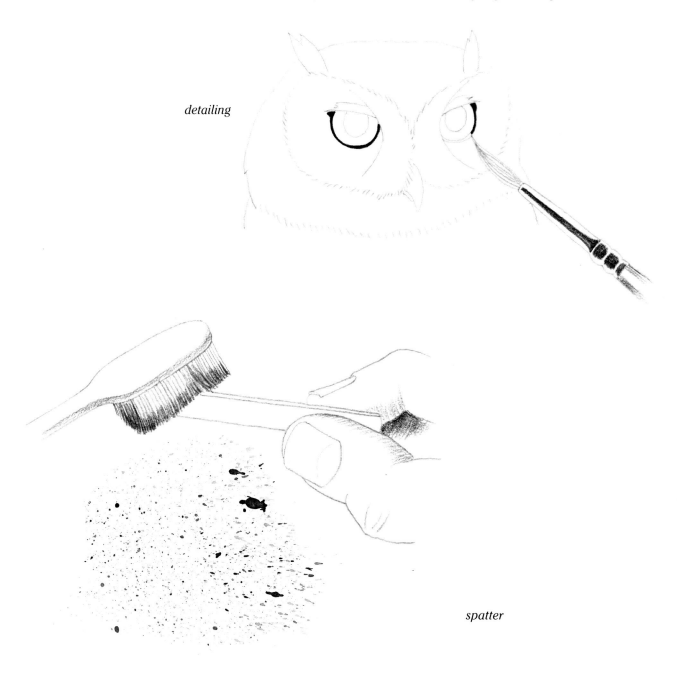

detailing

spatter

5
Putting the Techniques Together

Although not all the techniques previously described are used in any one bird painting, many can be. The following example employs a wide variety of these techniques, including tipping, splitbrush, detailing, and dry blending. It also demonstrates the use of transferring and liquid masking.

Because the screech owl's breast has several areas of white, the same color as the painting surface, it was necessary to put on a thin color wash to separate the bird from the background. The painting was done with gouache on cold press watercolor board, using #1 and #2 Kolinsky rounds and #4 filbert brushes for the bird and a 1½-inch sableline wash brush for the background wash. (The #2 round is used except where otherwise noted.)

A finished screech owl drawing on tracing paper is prepared for transfer by rubbing the reverse side with graphite.

At this time, only the outline of the owl is transferred to the board and the area to be left white is coated with masking fluid.

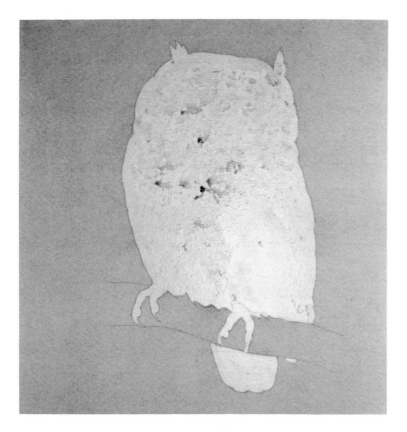

The board is moistened thoroughly using a spray mister and the clean wash brush to spread the water evenly. Then, a thin wet-in-wet background wash is applied with the 1½" brush loaded with thinned paint. The transferred outline of the branch may be seen through the wash.

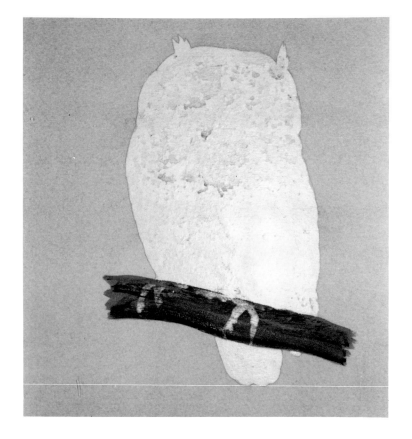

After the wash is dry, and before the masking is removed, the branch is painted in by applying a thin base color and drybrushing a darker color over it to add texture.

After the branch is dry, the masking is rubbed off. The tracing is then carefully repositioned over the white area and the details of the drawing are transferred.

A very thin wash of black is painted over the inner facial disc, throat, and undertail, and under the wing. An additional wash of the base body color is painted over the head, wing, and back.

Opaque black is painted on the bill, claws, eyes, and ruff. The breast is covered with opaque white.

Varying degrees of tipping—pressing and pulling with the filbert—produce different types of feather marks on the head and throat. Shading and suggestions of feather ends are lightly splitbrushed on the breast and belly.

The #1 round brush is loaded with opaque white and used to detail the inner facial disc feathers. These feathers are brushed rather loosely to allow some of the black underpainting to show through as shadows. A slightly darker color is used to paint the rest of the facial disc in the same manner. Opaque black is used in the splitbrush to make the dark breast patterns, carefully following the body contours.

The splitbrush is filled with color and the breast patterns are further refined. The basic foot color is painted in. Opaque black is used to detail the tiny dark pattern on the crown.

Opaque black is used in the #1 round to detail the edges of the ear tufts (hornlike feathers), wing, and tail. A thin black line is painted under the wing and wet blended into the white of the breast to separate the wing from the body. (If acrylics are used, the glazing technique is employed to blend the black line over the white, not into it.) Opaque black shadows are painted at the top of the eyelid and at the bottom of the belly where the feathers meet.

Opaque white is used to detail the breast feathers puffing over the top of the wing and to show the patterns on the wing feathers. White is also used with the splitbrush to indicate feather direction on the tail feathers, and with the #1 round to place rough highlights on the claws and bill. The iris of the eye is painted in with opaque color.

The rough black shadow previously painted at the top of the eyelid is blended with a clean, damp brush to soften it; the coarse white highlights on the claws and bill are softened in the same manner. (If acrylics are used, the bill and claw highlights must be softened while the white is still wet.) A light shadow is detailed on the tail feathers. A coarse, dark shadow is painted on the top of the eye.

The shadow at the top of the eye is dry blended down into the iris color. Tiny dark shadows are detailed onto the throat feathers. Finally, an opaque white highlight is added to the eye, and the screech owl is complete.

6
Describing
Owls

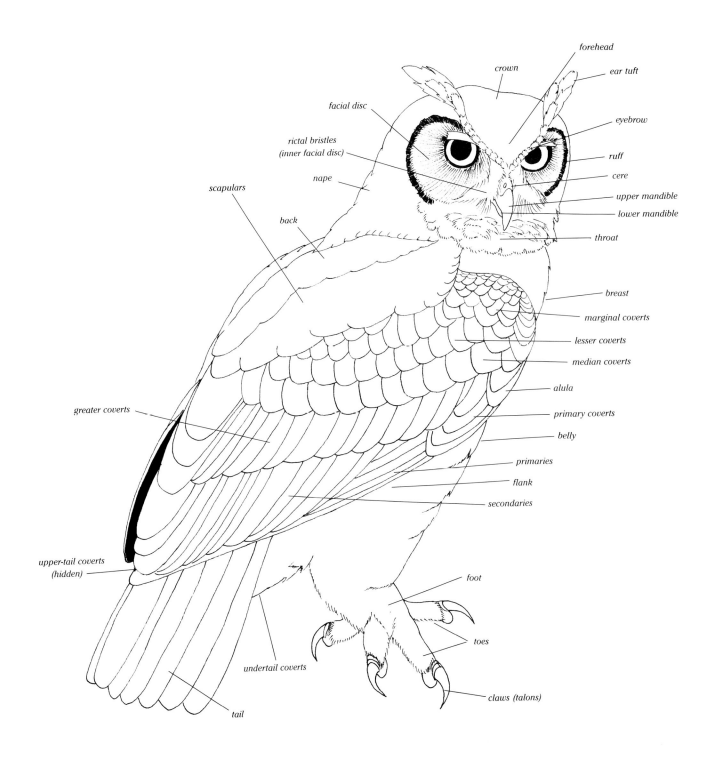

forehead

crown

ear tuft

facial disc

eyebrow

rictal bristles
(inner facial disc)

ruff

cere

nape

upper mandible

scapulars

lower mandible

back

throat

breast

marginal coverts

lesser coverts

median coverts

alula

primary coverts

greater coverts

belly

primaries

flank

secondaries

upper-tail coverts
(hidden)

foot

toes

undertail coverts

claws (talons)

tail

Although they have the same basic body features as other birds, owls exhibit a few adaptations—in eye location, feather form, bill shape, and toe arrangement—that enable them to live successfully in their environment. Knowledge of these special characteristics is essential to successful owl painting. This chapter will discuss the features common to most owls to help you become familiar with them.

Body Feathers

The body of a bird is covered with feathers that fall into groups with specific names. These names are important for identification and for descriptive purposes in following the steps in the painting examples.

The general appearance of owl feathers is very soft and puffy, with wing and body feathers adapted for virtually silent flight. They have predominantly muted colors and irregular patterns, which, while presenting problems for the artist, enable them to blend in well with their surroundings, both day and night. Owls' feathers provide protection from the elements as well as from enemies; when fluffed, they trap and hold air, providing additional insulation from the heat or cold. This puffing causes a noticeable change in the contours of the bird, making it seem more plump than normal.

An owl's state of excitement will also affect its shape. A relaxed owl sits with its ear tufts pointing back or tucked against its head and its body feathers very loose. But when the owl is excited the ear tufts stand erect and the other feathers are held tight to the body, resulting in a much slimmer appearance. For example, an agitated screech owl—normally a plump-looking little owl—extends its ear tufts as far as possible and holds its feathers very tight to its

screech owl "hiding"

screech owl relaxed

body in an attempt to become a rigid part of the landscape.

The facial disc is made up of various feather groups, most of which radiate from around the eye. The facial disc feathers help direct sound toward the ears, which are located just behind and under the disc. (The ear tufts on top of the head are modified head feathers and have nothing to do with hearing.)

Feet and Legs

To look at a perching owl, with only its toes and claws protruding from the belly feathers, you would think that the legs would be rather short. This, however, is not the case. The heavily feathered legs are actually quite long but are bent up and hidden by the body feathers, as is most of the feathered foot. The exceptions are the barn owl and burrowing owl. These two owls have rather long, exposed legs and feet with relatively few feathers on them.

All owls have four toes: two that point forward, one that points backward, and an outer toe that may point forward, backward, or sideways. When an owl is attacking its prey, the outer toe always points backward. The claws or talons at the end of the toes are quite formidable; they are well suited for grasping and holding prey.

When painting owl feet, at least two toes per foot should be pointing forward. Proper placement of the feet in relation to the body is crucial to achieving a balanced look.

Bills

The hooked bill is another specialized adaptation of owls, well designed for its task of tearing flesh. The upper mandible, which is fused to the skull, plunges into the prey; the mobile lower mandible does the holding and shearing. The basic shape of the bill is quite consistent among the different owl species, with some variations in length and degree of curvature. The tip of the bill comes to a point but is not needle sharp, and the top ridge of the bill is rounded. The base of the bill where it meets the skull is partially wrapped with a dense membrane called the *cere*, which surrounds the nostrils. Most of the bill is hidden by the inner facial disc feathers that protrude over and around it. Because the bill and eyes are in such close proximity, they are shown together in the accompanying illustration.

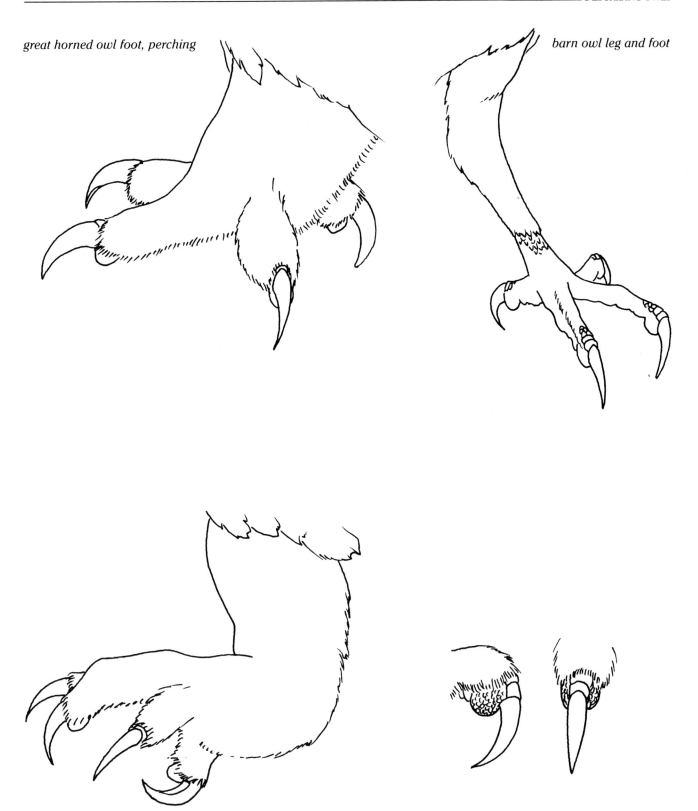

great horned owl foot, perching

barn owl leg and foot

great horned owl leg and foot, extended

typical owl claw

Eyes

A thin color (the iris color) is washed in, and the bill is painted with opaque color. The pupils are painted in opaquely and a dark shadow is placed at the top of each eye. Opaque white highlights are detailed on the bill. The eye ring is painted with opaque color, and the eye shadow and bill highlights are softened. An opaque highlight is added to the eye for a more lifelike appearance.

The placement of an owl's eyes is unique among birds: they are located at the front of the head, permitting binocular vision. The eyes are quite large and are convex—the eye protrudes into the skull as well as curving outwards. Owl eyes look expressive. When the lids are partially closed the owl has a sleepy, beatific look, but when they're open completely—as when the owl is excited—they have a wide-eyed, surprised appearance. As with all birds, owls cannot move their eyes in their sockets; it is therefore essential when painting to place the pupil in the center of the eye. (Owls are able to rotate their heads in all directions, including upside down, to compensate for this limitation.) Another consideration in painting an owl's eyes: the pupils should not be the same size if one eye is in light while the other is in less light or shadow.

Wings

Wings are yet another specialized area in owls. The noise of a bird in flight is made by air rushing over the wing. Because owls depend on silent flight for hunting, their wing feathers possess certain features that reduce wind noise. The first few primaries are soft on the trailing edges but have tiny curved projections on the leading edges; this combination helps reduce noise by interrupting the turbulent flow of air over the wing.

Although the various parts of the wing are easy to see in a schematic drawing, these feather groups tend to blend together on a living owl, and can be quite difficult to distinguish.

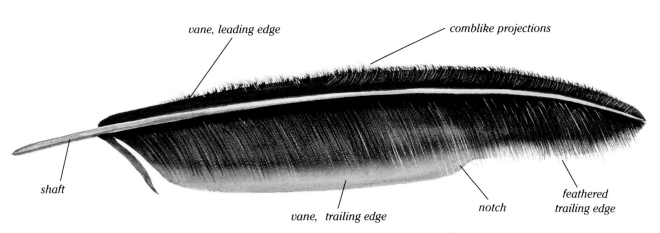

vane, leading edge

comblike projections

shaft

vane, trailing edge

notch

feathered trailing edge

Owl primary from leading edge of wing

Upper Wing

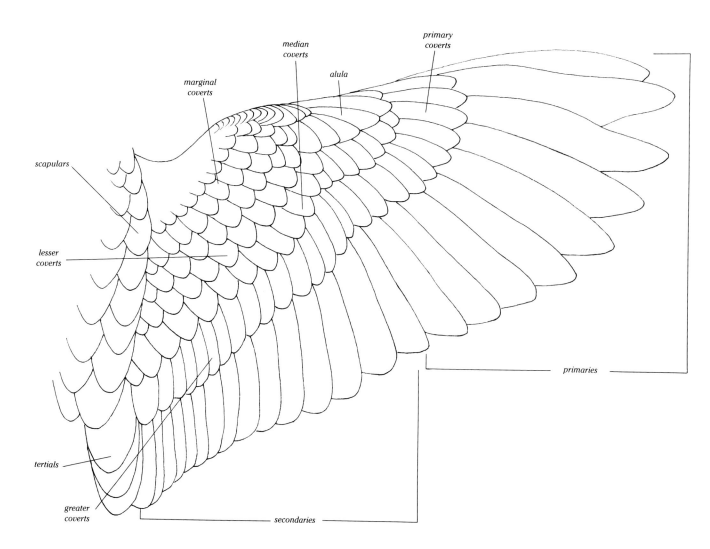

Underwing

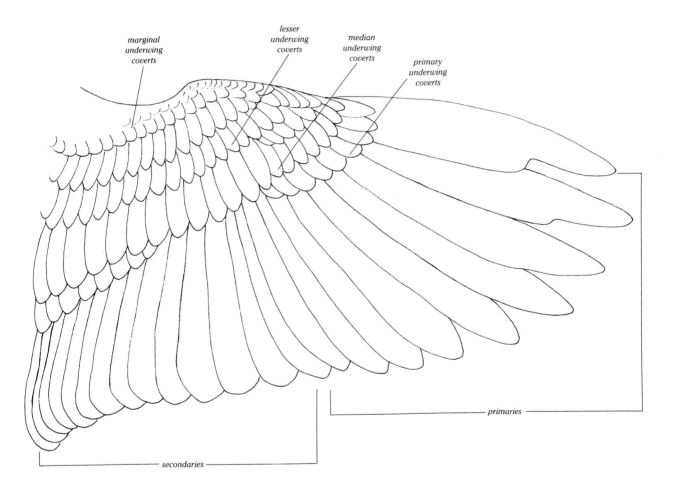

marginal
underwing
coverts

lesser
underwing
coverts

median
underwing
coverts

primary
underwing
coverts

primaries

secondaries

Tails

Probably the most neglected feather group, the tail is often obscured by a branch or covered by the folded wings. Nonetheless, the tail is very important because it is used extensively in flight, both as a rudder for turning and as a brake (especially when landing with one foot full of mouse). The tail is curved when viewed in profile, with the center feathers higher than the outer ones. The curvature is especially apparent with owls in flight. Owl tail feathers are usually short and quite broad.

7
Painting Examples

Painting Owls

Most owls have very muted coloration, thus only a few tubes of color are necessary in painting them. This does not mean that matching the color of owls is easy; on the contrary, the paints must be mixed very carefully to closely approximate the colors found in nature. Another difficulty is the variability of color and pattern within a species. For example, a great horned owl may have an overall appearance of brown, buff, or gray; the pattern on the breast may range from almost white with little barring to heavily barred with only a few white patches. This kind of shading and pattern variation occurs in most species of owls.

Drawings

Following the color painting examples are black-and-white line drawings of the individual owls. These are included to enhance your understanding of owls in various poses, ranging from the conventional to the unusual. When owls are viewed from these perspectives, with the coloration and pattern eliminated, the anatomical characteristics and relationships of the feather groups can be seen more clearly. These drawings are an excellent reference source: looking at them carefully will add to your knowledge of owls and help you achieve a more realistic owl painting.

Random Notes
Prior to Painting

As you follow along with the painting examples, you will notice that at times certain adjustments are made to the picture in color, value, shape, or whatever. This is the way a picture actually progresses; changes are always being made. These examples were not prepainted and then done again for this book. These are first-time examples, done so that you could see the real process of a bird picture being painted, corrections and all. Very little may be learned from watching the painting of a flawless picture.

Plan ahead when beginning a painting; have only those brushes, colors, and materials you will need at hand. Excess tubes, brushes and whatever only add clutter when you need it least. Although the colors on your palette look organized when first squeezed out, don't be dismayed when it all seems a mess after a short time. Very few artists maintain a controlled palette. Have a scrap of watercolor board handy to test brushes for load and stroke, and a rag or paper towel to blot brushes. Give yourself clean water, brushes, all the other painting stuff you'll need, and time to paint.

The following examples were done on cold press illustration board and the paints are gouache (designers colors). Winsor & Newton and Pelikan brands are used interchangeably, except in the case of raw umber, where the brand used will be noted. Pelikan raw umber has less yellow than does Winsor & Newton raw umber.

Though the examples are painted in gouache, the same techniques and colors may be used with acrylics with only a few adaptations in technique, which are noted in the text of the painting examples. Painting examples are not life-size.

Northern Saw-whet Owl

Aegolius acadicus

The muted coloration of the saw-whet owl allows it to remain hidden in a hollow tree or thicket of branches during the daylight hours. After dark, however, this tiny, robin-size owl ventures forth to stalk its prey as effectively as its larger kin. Insects and small rodents rustling on the forest floor attract the attention of this low-flying hunter; it swoops in quickly for the kill. These owls are actually quite common, but they are rarely seen because of their nocturnal habits and their ability to hide. When painting the saw-whet owl there are two distinct features that need to be captured: the wide-eyed, amazed look of its yellow eyes and the soft blending of its feathers. There is very little feather definition in this small owl. The total color impression of individual saw-whets can vary from a dark brown to a very light brown (the one illustrated here is a very light one).

The palette used is: ivory black, cadmium yellow pale, white, Pelikan raw umber, burnt umber, burnt sienna, yellow ochre, and violet. The brushes used are #4 sableline filbert, #3 Kolinsky sable round and sableline, and #1 Kolinsky sable round. Unless specifically noted, the #3 round is the brush used.

The completed drawing is transferred to the board. The lines are redrawn to intensify them so that they can be clearly seen through the washes that will be painted over them.

*Liquid masking is brushed over the
lower belly and foot where they
overlap the perch. After the masking
is dry, a thin wash of raw umber
and white is painted on the perch.
Thin black is washed on the facial
disc and throat.*

Black is drybrushed on the perch to add texture and used as a thin wash to add shading. A thin wet-in-wet wash of raw umber and burnt umber is painted over the top portion of the owl, including the wing and tail.

Masking is removed from the foot and belly. The #4 filbert is loaded with a mixture of raw umber, burnt umber, and a touch of black and used to tip in the dark ruff. The same mixture is splitbrushed to shade the forehead and nape, then used to paint feather edges on the back.

The preceding brown-black mixture
is then used to delineate the scapular, tail, and wing feathers. This
color is painted under each feather
and, while still wet, blended down
into the feather below with a clean
damp brush. This is a very time-
consuming procedure as it is done
one feather at a time.

A mixture of white, yellow ochre, and raw umber is splitbrushed on the scapulars and detailed on the edges of the wing feathers to give depth and roundness to the feathers.

An opaque mixture of white and yellow ochre is used to detail the edges of the nearest scapular feathers and the smaller wing coverts. A thin line of black is painted under the rest of the larger wing feathers and the tail feathers and wet blended into each feather to create a shadow. The bill is painted in with opaque black.

Opaque white is used to coat the lower body and foot, then split-brushed to create the pattern on the nape and blend the breast up into the black area of the throat. The opaque white is also used to detail the white patterns on the scapulars and wing feathers.

Black is splitbrushed on the lower body and breast to indicate shading and create a feathered look. An opaque mixture of yellow ochre and white is used in the #1 round to make the feathers on the facial disc, then painted on the bottom (fleshy part) of the hind toe. The #1 round is loaded with opaque white and the patterns on the ruff and forehead are painted in. A brush filled with clean water is used to blend the white feather patterns into the back and wing feathers. Opaque raw umber in the #1 round details the feather shafts on the smaller coverts.

Acrylic Note: The blending of the white feather patterns on the wing must be done while the white is still wet. Each feather is blended separately as the white is applied.

With a clean, damp brush, the black splitbrushing on the breast is blended up into the white breast. This softens the top and leaves clean dark strokes at the bottom. The opaque mixture of white and yellow ochre is used in the splitbrush to paint the tiny barbs on the outer ends of the facial disc feathers. The inner facial disc feathers and eye-brow are painted in with opaque white using the #1 round. These strokes are made rather loosely so that the black underpainting will show through as shadow areas. Opaque raw umber is splitbrushed on the crown.

Acrylic Note: The softening of the dark splitbrush strokes on the breast must be done as each is made.

Opaque black is splitbrushed around the eye and into the facial disc to indicate recessed shadow areas. A thinned mixture of burnt umber and burnt sienna is split-brushed over the white breast to show the feather pattern. Follow the body contours carefully to create the proper effect. If the thinned color mixture is not dark enough, splitbrush over the patterns again. Opaque black is splitbrushed on the foot to indicate feathering. Black is also used in the #1 round to detail the shadow areas where the belly feathers overlap the foot and where the breast feathers overlap the top of the wing.

Opaque black is used in the #1 round to paint the hind claw, pupil, and ring around the eye. It is also used to detail the eyelid and to paint tiny shadow lines under the neck to separate it from the body. The #3 round is loaded with black and used to draw a line under the wing and over the tail to separate the wing from the body. Then a clean, damp brush is used to wet blend the black down into the white and over the tail.

Acrylic Note: The same technique is used with acrylics, except the black is pulled down and glazed over the white, not into it.

Opaque black is painted under the foot to make a small shadow, and raw umber is painted on the pad of the hind toe to create a rounded look. Opaque white is used to place coarse highlights on the bill and hind claw. Cadmium yellow pale is used opaquely to paint in the iris. Opaque raw umber is splitbrushed on the secondary coverts.

Violet is mixed with the cadmium yellow pale (complementary colors), painted at the top of the eye and blended down into the yellow. A clean, damp brush is used to blend and soften the rough white highlights on the bill and claw. Opaque white in the #1 round is detailed on the leading edge of the primary to show the tiny projections. Finally, a curved white highlight is placed on the eye to give the finished saw-whet owl life.

Acrylic Note: The white highlights on the bill and claw must be blended while still wet.

Northern Saw-whet Owl

Northern Saw-whet Owl

Short-eared Owl

Asio flammeus

Unlike most other owls, the short-eared owl surveys its kingdom during the daylight and twilight hours rather than at night. This makes it one of the most commonly seen owls. Resting in the grass or atop a fence post, it scans the fields for rodents of any sort. When it is not perching it flies to enlarge its hunting area, usually quartering into the wind with slow, gentle wing strokes. Its flight feathers are often more tattered than other owls' as a result of plunging after prey in the tall grass. Normally the ear tufts of the short-eared owl are held close to the head and are not visible. In the painting example here, however, the owl is agitated and the ear tufts are completely erect. This is a rather dark phase of the short-eared owl with very distinct feather patterns.

The palette used is: ivory black, Pelikan raw umber, cadmium yellow pale, violet, white, Payne's gray, and yellow ochre. The brushes used are #1 and #3 Kolinsky round sables. Unless specifically noted, the #3 round is the brush used.

The completed drawing is transferred to the board.

Thinned black is painted on the throat and inner part of the facial disc. Liquid masking is painted over the foot; after it is dry, a thin coat of Payne's gray is washed over the post.

Black is drybrushed over the gray on the post to create texture. A thin mixture of black and raw umber is washed wet-in-wet over the upper parts of the owl. This wash is done in sections (head, then neck, then back, then tail). This wash need not be even in tone since it is just a base color.

If the transferred feather lines do not show through after the dark wash is applied, reposition the tracing and transfer them again. The base body color, with more black added to it, is painted on each back, scapular, and wing feather, then blended wet-in-wet up into each feather, one at a time, to create a rounded look. (In this step only a few of the feathers have been done; the rest will be completed in the next step.) The liquid masking on the foot is removed.

The remainder of the wing is completed. The initial breast color is a mixture of white, raw umber, and yellow ochre. This color is painted down the breast toward the belly. Opaque white is painted up from the undertail coverts and belly toward the breast color till they meet; then they are blended by pulling the white into the breast color with a clean, damp brush.
Acrylic Note: With acrylics this blending can be accomplished by working quickly and blending the colors while they are still wet. An alternate blending technique would be to paint the entire under part white and let it dry. Then, starting at the top of the breast, pull the opaque buff color down the breast with a clean, wet brush, glazing and grading it over the white until there is less and less color and a blended effect is achieved.

An opaque mixture of yellow ochre,
white, and a very small amount of
raw umber is used with a variety of
techniques and brushes to paint
in the light feather pattterns. The #1
round details the facial disc color
and the forehead and ear tuft patterns. A splitbrush is employed for
the nape and back markings. The
wing spots and foot are painted with
the #3 round.

The forehead, crown, and ear tuft feathers are further defined by detailing with a mixture of black and raw umber in the #1 round. This mixture is then splitbrushed on the brown areas of the head, nape and throat. Do not cover the base color entirely; emphasize the dark streaks and let some of the lighter base color show. The same mixture is then splitbrushed on the light underparts to show the dark feather patterns. Be careful to follow the body contours to create the proper feathered look. Tiny feathers are painted on the small throat area under the bill with an opaque mixture of white, yellow ochre, and raw umber.

Raw umber mixed with white is splitbrushed on the exposed primaries to lighten them. A thin black line is painted under each tail feather and then wet blended down into the feather below. Opaque raw umber is splitbrushed on the foot to create a feathered look. The facial disc is refined by splitbrushing out from the dark areas into the light areas with thinned black.

White, raw umber, and black are mixed and painted opaquely on the eyelids and toe pads. Thin black is lightly splitbrushed on the undertail coverts and belly. The white, yellow ochre, and raw umber mixture is used opaquely in the splitbrush on the primary tips to create a worn look. The same mixture is then used in the #1 round to paint the patterns on the tail, and to detail light feather edges on some wing coverts and tertials. It is then thinned and used in the #1 round to detail the shafts on the wing feathers.

Opaque black is painted on the claws and bill and detailed under the foot to create a shadow.

Then the #1 round is loaded with black and used to detail various shadow areas. Shadow lines are painted under the tertials, secondaries, and secondary coverts. Tiny black shadows are painted to sepa-rate the head from the nape, the nape from the back, and the scapulars from the wing. Black is also detailed at the top of the wing to show it tucking under the breast feathers, and at the top of the eyelids. Very thin black is splitbrushed over the median coverts.

The hard black shadow under the foot is dry blended with a clean, damp brush, and thin black is used to paint a shadow under each claw. Opaque black details the pupil and eye ring. Coarse opaque white highlights are painted on the claws and bill.
Acrylic Note: The black shadow under the foot must be blended while still wet.

A black line is painted under the wing and wet blended into the white with a clean, damp brush. White highlights on bill and claws are softened by dry blending. The #1 round is loaded with opaque white and used to further define the facial disc feathers around the bill. Opaque cadmium yellow pale colors the iris. Acrylic Note: The opaque highlights must be blended individually while still wet. The black shadow line under the wing is thinned and glazed over the white, not into it.

Opaque black in the #1 round details the nostrils and adds random feather breaks. Payne's gray is used in the #1 round to paint a fleshy ring around the eye. Violet is mixed with cadmium yellow pale (complementary colors), painted at the top of each eye, and wet blended down into the iris. A curved, opaque white highlight is placed in the eye and the short-eared owl is ready to take flight.

Short-eared Owl
(agitated)

Short-eared Owl
(relaxed)

Barn Owl

Tyto alba

Although it occasionally makes its home in a hollow tree, the barn owl seems to prefer the rural buildings of man for its roosting and nesting sites. The destruction, from decay or urban development, of old houses, barns, silos, and abandoned structures has severely cut into the preferred nesting areas of barn owls and reduced their range. Even at the height of their population barn owls were seldom seen because of their completely nocturnal habits. They are efficient hunters; their presence in an area can make a large dent in the rodent population.

A barn owl is strange looking, with a large head, heart-shaped facial disc, protruding bill, and long legs. Its feathers, however, have a very soft look, and their coloration is beautiful. This combination of distinct appearance, feather arrangement, and coloration makes the barn owl one of the most difficult owls to paint.

The palette used is: raw sienna, Pelikan raw umber, burnt sienna, yellow ochre, white, ivory black, and Payne's gray. The brushes used are a #4 sableline filbert and #1 and #3 Kolinsky sable rounds. Unless noted otherwise, the #3 round is the brush used.

The completed drawing is transferred to the board.

The feet are painted over with liquid masking. After it dries a thin wash of raw umber and yellow ochre is painted over the stump. A very thin wash of black is painted over the facial disc.

Opaque raw umber is drybrushed over the base color of the stump to add texture. A thin wash of black is painted on the underside of the tail and far wing. A wet-in-wet wash of raw sienna, yellow ochre, and white is painted over the head, nape, and back.

The masking is removed from the feet. A mixture of burnt sienna, raw sienna, and white is washed wet-in-wet over the wing and painted on the ruff of the facial disc. The same mixture is painted on the top of the back and wet blended into the back color to give the back roundness. Opaque white is painted over the lower part of the body and the legs.

Dark feather patterns on the wing are detailed with black in the #1 round. A mixture of white and yellow ochre is painted on the edges of a few coverts near the leading edge of the wing. Thin white is washed over the exposed primaries. Opaque white is painted on the first four or five secondaries. The opaque white is also used in the splitbrush to begin developing the facial disc featheration.

An opaque mixture of raw umber and yellow ochre is splitbrushed on the head, neck, and back, and on the leading edges of selected wing feathers. A very thin black wash is glazed over the coverts closest to the back. Thin black is also coarsely splitbrushed on the white underparts. A thin mixture of white, yellow ochre, and a tiny amount of raw umber is splitbrushed on various areas of the white underparts to add a blush. The degree and location of this blush color varies greatly from owl to owl.

With a clean, damp brush the split-brushing done on the breast in the previous step is softened by gently brushing the colors into the white. The undertail coverts are darkened with thin black to better separate them from the belly. Opaque white is painted on the outer edge of each tail feather and wet blended into the gray. The leading edge of the far wing is treated in the same manner. The underside of the primary is splitbrushed with opaque white. White and black are used in the #1 round to complete the patterns on the wing coverts. The bill is painted with a mixture of raw umber, white, and yellow ochre.

Acrylic Note: The splitbrushing on the breast must be blended with a clean, damp brush while it is still wet.

A thin black shadow line is painted under each primary and secondary wing feather and is wet blended down into each feather with a clean, damp brush. Opaque black is detailed to show the underside of the primary on the near wing and the underside of the covert on the far wing. The tail and far-wing primary feather shafts are detailed with white, then the splitbrush is used with opaque black to indicate detail on the feather vanes. The tip of the brush is split slightly and filled with opaque black to paint the dark feathers on the buff upperparts.

It is determined there is not enough separation between the far wing and the body, so the area next to the body is darkened with black and wet blended into the white. A thin black line is painted under the near wing and wet blended into the white underparts. Black is loaded in the #1 round and used to detail tiny shadow lines along the feather shafts and to darken the shadows between the tail feathers. Very thin black is selectively glazed over the legs and belly to emphasize shadow areas. Feet are roughed in with a mixture of black, white, and raw umber. A mixture of yellow ochre and raw umber is painted on the covert of the far wing.

Acrylic Note: When the thin black line is painted under the near wing it is blended down and glazed over the white with a clean, damp brush.

Opaque white is used in the #1 round to detail a white feather edge on the primaries and white secondaries. In addition, the white further defines the feathers of the facial disc, details the feather pattern on the crown, and indicates tiny white feathers on the legs and feet. Opaque white in the splitbrush emphasizes and highlights the pure white areas of the white underparts.

Opaque black in the #1 round is used to complete the dark patterns on the wing and tail feathers. Black is also splitbrushed on the facial disc to show shadow areas. An opaque mixture of burnt umber and burnt sienna is splitbrushed to show the rusty color on the facial disc. This mixture is also used in a #4 filbert to tip on the feathers on the ruff. The bottom feathers of the outer disc are opaque raw umber. Thinned black is painted on the shadow areas of the toes.

An opaque mixture of yellow ochre and white is loaded in the #4 filbert and tipped on the dark ruff, giving light tips to these feathers. The dark shadow areas of the facial disc are lightened and blended by stroking them with a clean, damp brush. The upper mandible is shaded with raw umber and the lower mandible with black. Black is also used for the nostril. The claws, a few scales on the toes, and the coarse shadows under the toes are painted in with opaque black. The tip of the #3 round is loaded with black and split slightly to brush the dark feather patterns onto the white underparts.
Acrylic Note: The splitbrushed shadow areas of the facial disc must be blended while the shading is still wet.

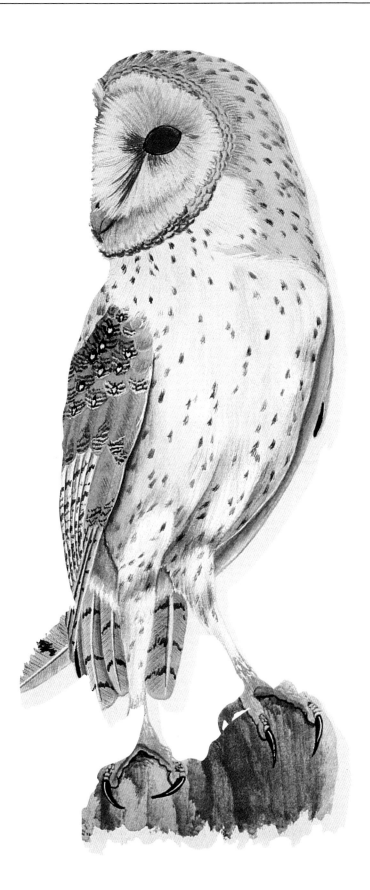

Opaque raw umber is used to paint the eye. The facial disc is refined with additional opaque white, which is also used to detail coarse highlights on the bill and claws. The outer part of the eye is detailed with opaque black. Dilute Payne's gray is dabbed on the toes to indicate scales. The black under the toes is blended down into the stump. The dark shaded areas on the belly and legs are defined and given a feathered look by light splitbrushing with thin black.

Acrylic Note: The black under the toes must be blended while the paint is still wet.

Opaque black paints in the pupil and darkens the iris until only a small amount of brown shows in the iris. Payne's gray is used in the #1 round to detail a thin gray line around the eye. Black in the split-brush darkens the facial disc at the top of the eye. The white highlights on the claws and bill are dry blended on their edges. Black is used in the #1 round to paint shadows under the claws, and thin shadows where the back overlaps the wing and where the breast feathers overlap the top of the wing. Opaque white is used in the #1 round to show the feathered leading edge of the primary. Finally, the white highlight is placed in the eye and the barn owl is complete. *Acrylic Note: The white highlights on the claws and bill must be blended while still wet.*

Barn Owl

Barn Owl

8
Practice Birds

Snowy Owl

Nyctea scandiaca

The only white North American owl, the snowy owl is a very large and powerful bird. Its normal range is in the far north, but it will venture south when there is a shortage of food. The degree of black marking is greater in immatures and females, while adult males may be almost completely white. This may appear to be a rather easy owl to paint because it is just white with black markings. This is not the case, however—the form of the owl must be shown with subtle shadings to give dimension and separation.

Palette: white, ivory black, Payne's gray, Pelikan raw umber, cadmium yellow pale, violet, ultramarine blue pale.

Snowy Owl (Rod Planck photo)

1. The entire owl is painted in with opaque white. The major body areas are shaded with a thin mixture of Payne's gray and ultramarine blue pale. This mixture is blended and glazed over the white until the desired effect is achieved.

2. The black pattern on the wing feathers is quite obvious. The trick here is the shading, which is done with the mixture of Payne's gray and ultramarine blue pale. The shading is detailed and splitbrushed in; it must not be overdone. In sidelight there is some separation between the feathers, but not great demarcation. In very flat light, such as an overcast day, the feathers blend together, with very little separation between them.

3. The breast and belly patterns are detailed in with opaque black. Where the shadows are deeper on the belly, undertail coverts, and tail, thinned black mixed with Payne's gray is used for the shading.

4. The puffiness of the breast is indicated with the blue and gray mixture in the splitbrush. If the shading looks too heavy, opaque white may be splitbrushed back over it.

Snowy Owl

Great Horned Owl

Bubo virginianus

The great horned owl is one of the largest North American owls, and the most widespread in range. It is a night hunter, spending the daylight hours hidden in the deep recesses of a tall evergreen tree. When roosting it is usually hunkered down with only a couple of toes showing under the belly feathers. This owl may give an overall color impression ranging from gray to dark brown to a buff-brown, which is the color painted here. The amount of white and black and the degree of barring on the underparts may vary greatly from one bird to another. The patterns on the back, scapular, and wing feathers are extremely irregular, so each feather is different from all the others. The owl pictured here is very alert, with feather tufts, body, and feathered legs extended.

Palette: Pelikan raw umber, burnt umber, yellow ochre, ivory black, white, cadmium yellow pale, violet.

Great Horned Owl (Gijsbert van Frankenhuyzen photo)

1. The buff-brown base color for the upper portions is a wet-in-wet thin mixture of raw umber and yellow ochre.

2. The facial disc feathers are an opaque mixture of burnt umber and raw umber tipped with black for the ruff. The eyes are cadmium yellow pale, shaded with a mixture of cadmium yellow pale and violet.

3. The back and wing feathers are painted with the base buff-brown color, then the pattern is detailed with white and black. The patterns shown are general—there is no consistency in the patterns.

4. The feathered legs and feet are painted with a mixture of yellow ochre, burnt umber, and white. The highlights and patterns are splitbrushed.

5. The breast is painted in with opaque white. The dark shading and blush color are splitbrushed using very thin colors. The black pattern is detailed on.

6. The throat is an opaque mixture of burnt umber, raw umber, and a small amount of white.

Great Horned Owl

Great Horned Owl

Burrowing Owl

Athene cunicularia

The burrowing owl makes its home underground in the abandoned holes of other animals. This habit is significant in painting this small owl because the feathers are often tattered from going in and out of its nesting place. Also, its habitat of prairies or treeless open country must be taken into consideration for the background. Its general appearance is of a dark little owl; the breast may be lighter or darker than the one pictured here. It has no ear tufts, and its wide yellow eyes with white eyebrows give it a perpetually annoyed look. The long legs appear to be bare, but they actually have a light covering of tiny feathers, with some skin color showing through. The transition of feathers on the breast from mostly dark to mostly light is quite abrupt. The tail is very short and nondescript.

Palette: Pelikan raw umber, ivory black, white, yellow ochre, cadmium yellow pale, violet, ultramarine blue pale.

Burrowing Owl (David Mohrhardt photo)

1. The base dark brown color for the entire owl is raw umber; it is applied in wet washes on the head, back, and wing. The tiny white marks on the crown are split-brushed.

2. The breast is painted with the raw umber, then the white pattern is splitbrushed on.

3. The belly is base painted with white and the raw umber pat-terns are splitbrushed on. The buff blush on the belly and legs, a mixture of yellow ochre and a tiny amount of raw umber, is also splitbrushed on.

4. The basic leg color is an opaque mixture of ultramarine blue pale, black, and white. This mix is also used for the bill.

5. The secondary coverts are quite simple: raw umber with white markings detailed on them.

6. The remainder of the coverts are painted in the same manner as the secondary coverts. The edges are detailed with white and raw umber mixed.

7. The eyes are opaque cad-mium yellow pale, shaded at the top with a violet and cadmium yellow pale mixture. The base brown color of the facial disc is raw umber mixed with white.

Burrowing Owl

Burrowing Owl

Barred Owl

Strix varia

One of the most common eastern owls, the barred owl is a quiet forest dweller. These owls are not as wild as other owls and may be approached quite closely. This trait is sometimes rather unfortunate since it makes them easy targets for misguided hunters. This medium-sized owl with no ear tufts has a rather nonchalant, easy air about it. It moves its head slowly to keep track of its surroundings. The barred owl has excellent daylight vision with its dark brown, black-looking eyes. The overall appearance may be gray-brown, reddish-brown, or dark brown with distinct lighter-colored markings. The breast pattern changes abruptly from crosswise to streaking on the belly. The pose painted here is very typical, with the owl relaxed and the belly feathers covering the whole foot except a couple of claws.

Palette: burnt umber, Pelikan raw umber, yellow ochre, ivory black, white.

Barred Owl (Larry West photo)

1. The base brown body color is a wet-in-wet wash of burnt umber and raw umber. The pattern on the head is opaque white with opaque raw umber splitbrushed.

2. The throat and upper breast patterns are an extension of the basic head pattern, with the raw umber splitbrushing extending over the white feather tips.

3. The belly is washed in with white; the dark patterns are detailed with raw umber. The shading is thinned black, lightly splitbrushed.

4. The patterns on the primaries and secondaries are detailed over the base body color with an opaque mixture of yellow ochre, white, and raw umber.

5. Opaque white is used to detail the pattern on the coverts. Raw umber is splitbrushed over the edges of the feathers to create shading.

6. The bill is yellow ochre and white.

7. The facial disc is splitbrushed white over a dark background. The pattern on the disc is raw umber tipped in with the splitbrush.

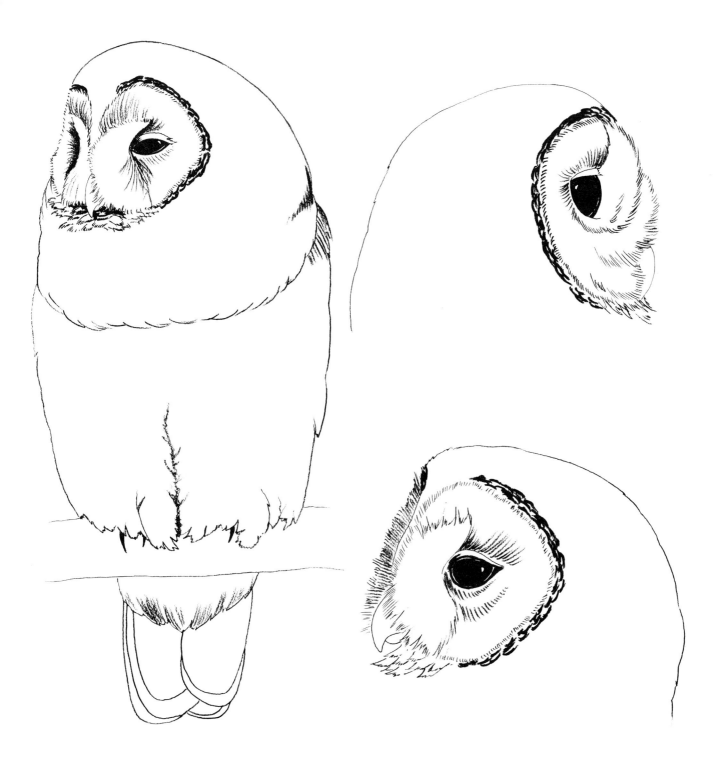

Barred Owl

Barred Owl

Screech Owl

Otus asio

Often nesting in hollow trees, the screech owl is commonly found in suburban as well as rural areas. Though this small owl is strictly a night hunter, it may frequently be seen in the daytime, roosting in the bright, warming sunlight. It is the only North American owl with two distinct color phases, gray and red. The red phase may occasionally be more brown than red. As with most owls the amount of pattern on the underparts may vary greatly. The gray phase has many more intricate patterns on the back, scapular, and wing feathers than does the red, where there are few patterns and the feathers tend to blend together. The screech owl painted here is the true red phase.

Palette: burnt sienna, burnt umber, ivory black, raw sienna, white, yellow ochre, Pelikan raw umber, cadmium yellow pale, violet.

Screech Owl (Larry West photo)

1. The base reddish color for the upper parts is a thin wet-in-wet mixture of burnt sienna and burnt umber. The feathers of the crown are tipped in with a filbert filled with opaque burnt umber.

2. The scapulars next to the wing have a definite pattern of white, black, and the base body color. The wing coverts are shaded with splitbrushed burnt umber.

3. The secondaries have a muted, dark pattern of a thin mixture of raw umber and burnt umber.

4. The breast is painted with opaque white. The light feather-edge shading is thinned black in the splitbrush. The colored pattern is the mixture of burnt sienna and burnt umber detailed to follow the contour of the bird. The center of the pattern is opaque black.

5. The throat is detailed over a light black wash with an opaque mixture of yellow ochre, white, and burnt umber.

6. The same mixture used on the throat is splitbrushed on the facial disc, again over a thin black wash. The eyes are cadmium yellow pale shaded with a yellow and violet mixture.

Screech Owl

9
Reference Material

A frequent problem bird artists have is in obtaining adequate reference material. Although there is no substitute for observing the colors, attitudes, postures, and habits of birds in the wild, other reference sources must be considered since few of us have the ability to remember the field marks, color, and shape of a particular bird well enough to paint it accurately in the studio. However, when examining several reference sources, especially photographs and printed material, for specific species of bird, you will notice wide variation in color for that bird from different sources. These color variations are due to many factors, ranging from the time of day a photograph was taken (flat midday light or warm afternoon light) to the accuracy of the printer in reproducing a color. The artist must choose his reference material carefully so that he can accurately portray the bird as he perceives it. The following are suggestions for sources of reference material.

Photographs. Most wildlife artists have a 35mm camera and telephoto lens to take their own reference photos of birds in the outdoors, whether in the wild or at the feeder. Original photos are an excellent source of material; however, they should be used as an aid, not as a crutch. Unfortunately, many bird artists rely exclusively on photographs they copy directly. Thus, their pictures are merely renderings of photographs—a far cry from original art.

Nature Centers, Sanctuaries, and Zoos. All these provide the opportunity to observe live birds, caged and free. Be aware that some physical features may be affected by captivity. Caged birds may have tattered wings and broken bills from flying against the cages. Also, some of the birds, especially at sanctuaries and nature centers, are brought in injured and could have broken wings or other disfiguring injuries that should be taken into account. Some loose yet captive birds are pinioned (wing tip removed) to prevent flight; this means there is only one complete wing. Though this reads like a list of horrors, such birds are well cared for and afford the artist an opportunity to closely observe some birds that are very difficult to see in the wild, even at a distance.

Books and Magazines. Both contain art and photographs that may be used for reference; most bird artists have files of material saved from magazines and other printed sources. There are scores of bird art books, some of which are useful sources of general reference. The rule here is: Don't use other artists' work as the *only* source of reference, for if an error was made in the original art, you will perpetuate it. Only use the art of others in conjunction with other reference material.

Preserved Specimens. Museums and nature centers usually have collections of preserved birds, as study skins, mounted in lifelike poses, or frozen, awaiting preparation. If you can gain access to these collections, they are excellent sources of reference material. The anatomical accuracy of mounted specimens may vary greatly, depending on how long the bird has been mounted and skill of the preparator. Again, there are things to be aware of. As soon as a bird dies, even if it is frozen immediately, it loses, for lack of a better term, its "life force." It becomes smaller as everything collapses, and colors begin to fade immediately, especially in the legs and bill. Road and window kills also suffer the loss of "life force" and fading. Additionally, there are state and federal laws governing the possession of owls, dead or alive, without a special permit. Before keeping any specimens, investigate local and federal laws with your state conservation department.

Carvers' Supply Sources. These stores sell feet, bills, and occasionally heads cast from actual owl specimens. A good reference source.

Falconers. Special permits allow falconers to keep and fly birds of prey. Many of these people have live, trained owls that make excellent reference sources. Check with a local nature center or bird sanctuary for names of falconers in your area.

Reference Books

Audubon Society. *Field Guide to North American Birds, Eastern Region.* New York: Alfred A. Knopf, 1977.

————. *Master Guide to Birding,* 3 Vol. New York: Alfred A. Knopf, 1983.

Austin, Oliver L. and Arthur Singer. *Birds of the World.* New York: Golden Press, 1961.

Burn, Barbara. *North American Birds,* The National Audubon Society Collection Series. New York: Bonanza Books, 1984.

Carlson, Kenneth L. and Laurence C. Binford. *Birds of Western North America.* New York: Macmillan Publishing, 1974.

Casey, Peter N. *Birds of Canada.* Ontario: Discovery Books, 1984.

Eckert, Allan W. *The Owls of North America.* New York: Doubleday & Co., 1974.

Ede, Basil. *Basil Ede's Birds.* New York: Van Nostrand Reinhold, 1981.

Epping, Otto M. and Christine B. Epping. *Eye Size and Eye Color of North American Birds.* Winchester, Va.: Privately printed, 1984.

Gromme, Owen J. *Birds of Wisconsin.* Madison: The University of Wisconsin Press, 1974.

Holt, T. F. and S. Smith, eds. *The Artist's Manual.* New York: Mayflower Books, 1980.

Hosking, Eric. *Eric Hosking's Birds.* London: Pelham Books, 1979.

Jeklin, Isidor and Donald E. Waite. *The Art of Photographing North American Birds.* British Columbia: Whitecap Books, 1984.

Johnsgard, Paul. *North American Owls.* Washington, D.C.: Smithsonian Institution Press, 1988.

Lansdowne, J. F. *Birds of the West Coast,* 2 Vol. Boston: Houghton Mifflin, 1980.

Lansdowne, J. F., with J. A. Livingston, *Birds of the Northern Forest.* Boston: Houghton Mifflin, 1966.

Lansdowne, J. F. and J. A. Livingston. *Birds of the Eastern Forest,* 2 Vol. Boston: Houghton Mifflin, 1970.

Mohrhardt, David. *Bird Reference Drawings.* Berrien Springs, Mich.: Oak Bluff Press, 1985.

———. *Bird Studies.* Berrien Springs, Mich.: Oak Bluff Press, 1986.

———. *Selected Bird Drawings.* Berrien Springs, Mich.: Oak Bluff Press, 1987.

Perrins, Christopher M. and Alex L. A. Middleton. *The Encyclopedia of Birds.* New York: Facts on File Publications, 1985.

Porter, Eliot. *Birds of North America.* New York: A & W Visual Library by E. P. Dutton.

Robbins, Chandler S. et al. *A Guide to Field Identification—Birds of North America.* New York: Golden Press, 1966.

Saitzyk, Steven L. *Art Hardware.* New York: Watson-Guptill, 1987.

Scott, Shirley L., ed. *Field Guide to the Birds of North America.* Washington, D.C.: National Geographic Society, 1985.

Terres, John K. *The Audubon Society Encyclopedia of North American Birds.* New York: Alfred A. Knopf, 1980.

Tunnicliffe, C. F. *A Sketchbook of Birds.* New York: Holt, Rinehart and Winston, 1979.

———. *Sketches of Bird Life.* London: Victor Gollancz Ltd., 1981.

———. *Tunnicliffe's Birds.* Boston: Little, Brown and Company, 1984.

Glossary

Acrylic Gesso. An acrylic polymer emulsion that can be either white or gray/black and serves as a ground for acrylic paints. This is not a true gesso as is used in oil painting.

Acrylic Paints. Pigments that are bound together with synthetic resins or polymer emulsions. Water based, they dry fast and hard and are not water-soluble when dry.

Binder. The substance used to coat and hold pigment in suspension and bind the pigment particles together when dry.

Blending. Bringing the edges of two colors together and mixing them to form a smooth transition rather than a hard line.

Blends. The combination of synthetic filaments and natural hairs used in the manufacture of brushes.

Boards. Paperboards of varying thickness that have a drawing, painting, or colored paper adhered to one side. Illustration, watercolor, and mat boards are all paperboards.

Bristle. The stiff rigid body hair of hogs and pigs, characterized by split ends on each bristle.

Canvas. Any woven fabric used as a painting surface. The two most common fabrics are cotton and linen, and they are classified by thread count and ounces per square yard. The finest canvas available is made from Belgian linen.

Complementary Colors. Colors opposite one another on the color wheel that, when mixed together, have a neutralizing or toning-down effect on each other; for instance, to tone down a bright yellow, add a very small amount of violet. The diagram shows a simple color wheel with the primary colors—red, yellow, blue—and their complementary colors. Orange is the complement of blue, green of red, and violet of yellow.

Consistency of Paint. Refers to the viscosity—thickness or thinness—of paint.

Designers Colors. See Gouache.

Detailing. Painting fine-line details on a picture or carving.

Dimension. In painting, refers to shading that gives shape, separation, or roundness to a form.

Drybrush. The technique of painting with very little paint in the brush to produce broken irregular lines or shapes.

Earth Tones or Colors. Naturally occurring in organic pigments that contain clay or silica, they are processed and produce very permanent colors, such as raw umber and raw sienna.

Ferrule. The metal, plastic, or quill sheath that holds the hairs to the handle of a brush.

Filament. Any synthetic material used in the manufacture of artificial brush hairs.

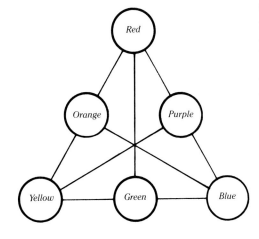

Filberts. Flat brushes that have rounded ends.

Finish. Describes the surface texture of a paper or board: hot press has a smooth finish, cold press has a medium finish, rough has an irregular finish.

Flats. Flat brushes with squared ends.

Flow Release. Synthetic or natural (ox gall) wetting agents that reduce the surface tension of paints, increasing their ability to flow evenly.

Frisket. See Masking.

Fugitive Colors. Colors which are not stable and that fade or disappear over time.

Gels. Thickening agents added to paints that increase the impasto effect.

Glazing. Painting a thinned color over a dry base color so that the two mix visually and some of the base color shows through.

Gouache *(Opaque Watercolor, Designers Colors).* A water-based opaque paint made with pigments, a gum binder, zinc white pigment, and other additives.

Grading. Creating a smooth transition from pure color to clear or no color.

Ground. A painting surface that serves as an absorbent stable base for the paint; for instance, acrylic gesso is a ground for acrylic paint.

Gum Arabic. A natural gum from the acacia tree, used as a binder for both gouache and transparent watercolor. It may also be added separately to give extra transparency.

Hair. Used in brushes, it is flexible and very absorbent. The amount of spring, absorbency, and shape depends upon the animal the hair is from.

Hardboard. A composition-wood fiber board used in the construction industry. In its untempered form it provides a good painting surface when prepared with a ground.

Highlight. To emphasize an area on a painting surface that would catch and reflect intense light.

Impasto. Paint applied thickly to give a three-dimensional quality.

Lifting Off. A subtractive technique of moistening and removing dry paint.

Load. The amount of paint carried in the hairs of a brush. A full load is when the hairs are thoroughly saturated but not dripping.

Masking. Blocking out an area with liquid masking or paper to form a barrier that does not allow paint to penetrate its surface.

Matte Finish. A flat nonglossy finish.

Medium. The material in which an artist works or which, as an additive, alters the materials.

Oil Paint. Pigments which use oils as a binder and require solvents and oils as thinning agents.

Opaque. The ability of a paint to cover a surface and not allow light to pass through it.

Opaque Watercolor. See Gouache.

Ox Gall. See Flow Release.

Ox Hair. Blunt hair from ox ears. Used in brushes, it is dyed red and called sableline.

Palette. Any surface used to hold concentrated paint for paintings. Also the selection of colors used in a certain painting.

Permanence. The degree of light-fastness of a color, the longevity of which depends upon many factors, including ingredients used in manufacturing, light, humidity, and pollutants.

Pigment. Coloring matter that is derived from natural or synthetic sources. Also used as a synonym for paint or color.

Premixed Colors. Shades of colors mixed by the manufacturer.

Retarder. An additive that slows the drying time of paints.

Round. The most commonly used watercolor-brush shape. The hairs are in a round ferrule and should come to a fine point.

Sable. Hairs in this category are from various members of the weasel family. They are generally characterized as having a fine point and great spring and strength. Kolinskys are the finest hairs in this group; they come from the Asian mink found in Siberia.

Sableline. See Ox Hair.

Softening. Lightly brushing along the edge of a hard line to blend it slightly.

Soluble. Capable of being dissolved by a particular substance.

Spattering. Creating a random pattern of color spots or blobs, usually by snapping the bristles of a stiff brush held above the surface to be painted.

Splitbrush. Fanning the hairs of a brush until they split apart.

Tipping. Touching only the tip of a brush to a surface and lifting or dragging it to produce various marks.

Tone. General coloring of an area.

Tooth. The texture of a surface, whether paper or gesso, which influences how the paint will appear. A smooth surface has less tooth than does a rough surface.

Transfer. The act of transferring or duplicating a drawing from one surface to another.

Transparent. In painting, the quality of paint that allows light to pass through it.

Transparent Watercolor. A water-based paint with a high concentration of finely ground pigments in a gum arabic binder.

Visual Weight. The perceived impact, brightness, and depth of a color.

Wash. The application of paint thinly or transparently: may be a continuous (even) tone, graded, or glazed.

Watercolor Paper. Handmade or machine-made, a variety of fibers are used in its manufacture, including wood pulp, bark, cotton, and combinations of these. The finest papers are made from 100% cotton fibers.